Contents

Let's Cook!

Looking at Mexico

Mexico is a country made up of 31 states. It is the 14th largest country in the world and home to over 120 million people – and lots of delicious, spicy food!

NORTH AMERICA

Mexico

SOUTH AMERICA

Mexico is a country in Central America. The United States forms its border in the north. Belize and Guatemala form its southern border.

Viva México!

Officially called the United Mexican States, Mexico is a long, bent wedge shape of land with the Pacific Ocean to the west and the Gulf of Mexico and Caribbean Sea to the east. The country has dry deserts in the north, and major mountain ranges run up and down the length of the country. The tropical climate of the south is perfect for growing fruit and vegetables. Mexico has a long history with several great ancient civilizations, including the Olmec, Maya and Aztecs. Spain overthrew the last of these, the Aztec Empire, in 1521. However, the descendants of these people make Mexico the beautiful and fascinating land it is today. Many of their delicious foods have conquered the world. Viva México (Long live Mexico)!

 A tortilla wrap stuffed with meat and colourful vegetables is a staple food in Mexico.

4

Mexico

The Culture and Recipes of Mexico

Tracey Kelly

Raintree is an imprint of Capstone Global Library Limited, a company incorporated in England and Wales having its registered office at 264 Banbury Road, Oxford, OX2 7DY – Registered company number: 6695582

www.raintree.co.uk
myorders@raintree.co.uk

© Brown Bear Books Ltd 2017
This edition published by Raintree in 2020

Created by Brown Bear Books Ltd
Text and Editor: Tracey Kelly
Editorial Director: Lindsey Lowe
Children's Publisher: Anne O'Daly
Design Manager: Keith Davis
Designer: Melissa Roskell
Picture Manager: Sophie Mortimer
Production by Tori Abraham
Printed and bound in India

ISBN 978 1 4747 7848 0 (hardback)
ISBN 978 1 4747 7854 1 (paperback)

British Library Cataloguing in Publication Data
A full catalogue record for this book is available from the British Library.

Acknowledgements
We would like to thank the following for permission to reproduce photographs:
t=top, c=centre, b=bottom, l=left, r=right
Front Cover: Shutterstock
Inside: 123rf: Mike Flippo 15b, Wavebreak Media 30; Dreamstime: 19b, 25br, Kobby Dagan 28–29c, 31br, Dieter Hawlan 9bl, Jesse Kraft 36–37t, Lunamarina 6b, Anna Omelchenko 5br, Arturo Osorno 11br, William Perry 28–29t, Juan Manuel Robledo 39, Travelling Light 45br, Martyn Unsworth 22t; Getty Images: Steve Dunwell 28–29b, Arturo Lara 20–21b; Shutterstock: 7b, 8–9t, 17b, 23t, 27br, 32bl, 37, AS Food Studio 1cl, Kobby Dagan 20–21t, 22b, Konstantin Kopachinsky 41b, Rafal Kubiak 5bl, Anamaria Mejia 5tl, Monkey Business Images 38–39b, Tyler Olson 25bl, Lefteris Papaulakis 1blr, Marco Regalia 7t, Nancy Sullins 1cr, 6t, T Photography 38–39t, Tati Novo Photo 36–37b, Lilyana Vynogradova 43br, Yeko Photo Studio 4l; Thinkstock: istockphoto 8cr, 10–11t, 19b, 30–31b, 33t, 35br.
Special thanks to Klaus Arras for all other photography.

Every effort has been made to contact copyright holders of material reproduced in this book. Any omissions will be rectified in subsequent printings if notice is given to the publisher.

All the internet addresses (URLs) given in this book were valid at the time of going to press. However, due to the dynamic nature of the internet, some addresses may have changed, or sites may have changed or ceased to exist since publication. While the author and publisher regret any inconvenience this may cause readers, no responsibility for any such changes can be accepted by either the author or the publisher.

The land in northwest Mexico is mainly dry, barren desert. Cacti are among the few plants that grow here.

○ Tijuana

UNITED STATES

BAJA CALIFORNIA

SIERRA MADRE OCCIDENTAL

SIERRA MADRE ORIENTAL

Rio Grande

La Paz ○

Mazatlán ○

MEXICO

○ Monterrey

GULF OF MEXICO

CUBA

○ Tampico

Chichén Itzá ○ ○ **Cancún**

Teotihuacán

Guadalajara ○

○ **Mexico City**

YUCATÁN

○ Manzanillo

PACIFIC OCEAN

○ **Veracruz**

BELIZE

○ **Palenque**

Acapulco ○

○ **Oaxaca**

GUATEMALA **HONDURAS**

Teotihuacán, near Mexico City, is one of many ancient ruins in Mexico. No one is sure who built it.

Acapulco is a famous Mexican holiday resort. Tourists visit for its beaches, water sports and restaurants.

Desert land

Hot, dry desert covers much of Mexico. Located in the central northern part of the country, the Chihuahuan Desert stretches across the border with the United States. It covers a large area of 450,000 square kilometres (175,000 square miles). The Chihuahuan lies between the Sierra Madre Oriental and the Sierra Madre Occidental Mountains. Parts of it stretch into New Mexico and Texas. Other large deserts include the Coahuila Desert and Deserts of Nuevo León.

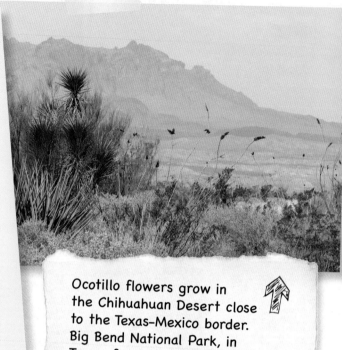

Ocotillo flowers grow in the Chihuahuan Desert close to the Texas–Mexico border. Big Bend National Park, in Texas, forms the backdrop.

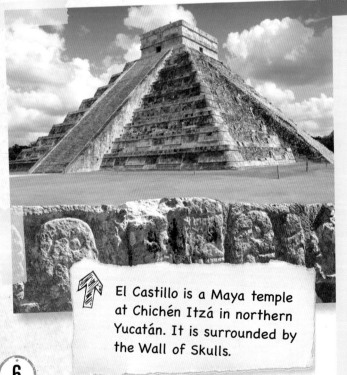

El Castillo is a Maya temple at Chichén Itzá in northern Yucatán. It is surrounded by the Wall of Skulls.

Ancient sites

The Yucatán peninsula was home to the Maya, one of Mexico's ancient civilizations that began to develop in central Mexico around 1500 BC. The Maya left behind a legacy of temples, palaces and plazas. Today, millions of people visit sites, such as the temples of Chichén Itzá, an astronomical observatory named El Caracol and the Pyramid of the Magician at Uxmal. They also visit Palenque, a major Maya city in southeastern Mexico.

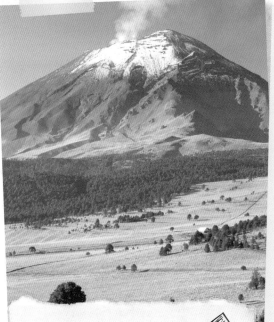

Popocatépetl is an active volcano that last erupted in 2016, spewing smoke and ash.

Mexican plain

Much of Mexico's industry and food production take place in the Central Plateau (Plain), which is shaped like an inverted triangle. Moving south from the top, the land is fertile and supports farming for the area's dense population. The country's capital, Mexico City, is located here. It is one of the world's largest cities and sits in a basin 2,250 metres (7,380 feet) high. Surrounded by mountains, pollution from cars and factories hangs in a blanket over the city. Popocatépetl, an active volcano 5,426 metres (17,802 feet) high, is located only 43 miles (70 kilometres) away. Its name is the Aztec word for "smoking mountain".

Mountains high

Rugged mountain ranges border the Central Plateau: the Sierra Madre Occidental to the west and Sierra Madre Oriental to the east. They join together near Mexico City. In the southwest, mountains are covered with pine and oak forests that belong to Native Americans who have lived in the region for thousands of years. Oaxaca has stunning mountains, rivers, canyons, waterfalls, hot springs and lagoons.

Beautiful mountain views can be seen from the hot springs at Hierve El Agua, rock formations in Oaxaca, in southern Mexico.

Let's Cook!

Food and Farming

Mexico produces plenty of fruit and vegetables and its own staple – corn. People also rear cattle and catch fish.

Cacao and maize

Chocolate and maize (also called corn) are among the top foods that Mexico has given the world! Centuries ago, Native Americans in Mexico farmed a wild grass named teosinte. Over time, they developed it into maize. Today, a favourite food is corn on the cob (the ear of a maize plant), sprinkled with lime and salt and grilled on a barbecue. Maize kernels can be dried and ground into masa harina flour, which is used for making tortillas. The cacao tree is native to Central America. Aztec and Maya peoples made a hot drink by mixing the dark, bitter chocolate from its seeds with honey and spices, and sweet chocolate was born! Spanish invaders took cacao seeds back to Europe, and chocolate spread across the world.

Cacao pods grow on branches. After being removed from the pods, cacao beans are dried and stored in hessian sacks.

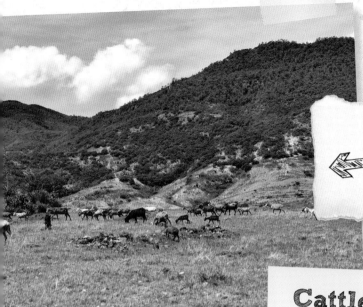

Lush, green pastures make good grazing for livestock in a valley in Oaxaca, in southern Mexico.

Cattle call

Mexico has a large amount of open grassland for herds of grazing animals. Cows, goats and sheep are reared to produce dairy products and meat. Animals are raised on the northern plain, in central Mexico and in the south. The Spanish conquerors were the first to bring cattle, pigs and horses to the country in the 1500s. Today, cattle ranching is one of the fastest-growing industries in Mexico. The country produces and exports large amounts of beef, and Mexicans themselves eat many beef dishes. Sadly, forests are being cleared to create even more pastureland for grazing, and this is destroying the delicate habitats of many native animal and bird species.

Small farms

Many farmers in central Mexico produce vegetables and fruit on small family farms. They grow maize, wheat, peanuts, chillies, squashes and beans using traditional farming methods. People buy and sell produce at busy markets in every town and village. In the cities, huge markets like Mexico City's historic La Merced Market sell fresh food to thousands of city dwellers.

DID YOU KNOW?

Native American people have grown maize for around 10,000 years. From Mexico, maize spread north to the United States and south to Peru. It is now the world's most widely grown staple food.

Tropical fruits, such as bananas, pineapples and peppers, fill a market stall with colourful, mouthwatering produce.

Tropical south

The south of Mexico and the Gulf Coast have a tropical climate, meaning that it is always hot and humid. Farmers grow coconuts, papaya, bananas, pineapple and mangoes. Sugar cane, coffee and cocoa beans are also important crops from the south, as well as the vanilla orchid, from which vanilla extract is made. Farmers in the Oaxaca region grow corn, beans, sugar cane, melons and citrus fruit. In the lowlands of the Yucatán Peninsula, rice, wheat, squash, chillies and tomatoes are grown, and bees produce delicious honey.

A papaya plantation stretches across the foothills in Colima, a state in western Mexico on the Pacific coast.

Big catches

With a vast 9,330 kilometres (5,800 miles) of coastline, fish and seafood are plentiful in Mexico. They are a key ingredient in the nation's cuisine. Along the coasts of the Gulf of Mexico, the Pacific Ocean and the Baja Peninsula, fishers catch lobster, shark, tuna, sardines, mackerel and other fish and shellfish. Shrimp, sea bass and shark are caught in the seas off the Yucatán Peninsula. Mexican fishers catch around 1.5 million tonnes of fish and seafood each year, and three-quarters of this is fished near Pacific ports such as Manzanillo, Mazatlán and Guaymas.

Fishers bring in their catch on a beach near the port of Veracruz, in east central Mexico.

Let's start cooking

One thing's for sure – cooking is a lot of fun! In this book, you will learn about different ingredients, which tastes go together and new cooking methods. Some recipes have steps that you'll need help with, so you can ask a parent or another adult. When your delicious meal is ready, you can serve it to family and friends.

This line tells you how many people the meal will feed.

Serves 4–6

In this box, you find out which ingredients you need for your meal.

YOU WILL NEED

- 140 g milk chocolate or plain chocolate (or half of each)
- 2 large eggs
- 15 g icing sugar

Before you begin, check that you have everything you need. Get all the ingredients ready before you start cooking.

WARNING!

When to get help

Most cooking involves chopping ingredients and heating them in some way, whether it's frying, boiling or baking. Be careful as you cook – and make sure your adult kitchen assistant is around to help!

TOP TIP
You can choose
any chocolate you like.

Top Tip gives you more information about the recipe or the ingredients.

How to chop an onion

For many meals, you need to chop an onion. Cut a thin slice off at both ends, then pull off the papery skin. Cut the onion in half down the middle. Put one half, cut side down, on the cutting board. Hold it with one hand, and cut slices with the other hand. Hold the slices together, then cut across them to make small cubes. Be careful not to cut yourself!

How to chop chillies

Some recipes use fresh chillies – and they are very hot! Chilli seeds and the white pith makes your skin burn, so always wear rubber or vinyl gloves when chopping chillies. If you don't have any gloves, wash your hands really well afterwards and do not touch your skin or eyes for a while. To chop, trim the chilli stalk, then halve lengthwise. Scrape out the seeds and throw away. Slice the stalk into fine pieces.

Oven temperature conversions

°C	°F	Gas Mark
140	275	1
150	300	2
170	325	3
180	350	4
190	375	5
200	400	6
220	425	7
230	450	8
240	475	9

Tasty tortillas

Makes 12 tortillas

Tortillas are a great, versatile food. You can buy them from a shop, but they are easy to make with this recipe.

YOU WILL NEED

- ✔ 300 g masa harina flour
- ✔ a pinch of salt
- ✔ about 360 ml hot water
- ✔ 5 g butter

1 In a large bowl, mix the masa harina flour with the salt. Bring the water to boil in a saucepan, and pour it over the masa harina, stirring as you pour. Put the butter in a frying pan over medium heat, and stir until it is melted. Pour it into the bowl with the flour.

2 Combine all the ingredients using a big wooden spoon. Be careful: it's very hot! Put the bowl to one side, and leave the dough until it is cool enough to touch.

DID YOU KNOW

Masa harina is a flour made from maize. You can buy it online if you can't find it in the shops.

TOP TIP

To store tortillas, put them in a covered dish in the fridge. They will keep for up to three or four days.

3 Using clean hands, knead the dough together, until it forms a large ball.

4 Divide the dough into 12 portions. To do this, first cut the ball in half, then cut each smaller ball in half again. Divide each of these four balls into three. Leave the dough balls for an hour.

5 Take a dough ball, and put it between two layers of plastic wrap. Then roll with a rolling pin, until you have a 15 cm circle. Pull off the plastic wrap, being careful not to tear the dough circle. Repeat with the other balls.

6 Heat the frying pan, and add a tortilla. You don't need to add any fat. Cook for 1 minute, then turn with a spatula, and cook the other side for 1 minute. Cook all the tortillas. Cover them with a clean tea towel to keep them warm, and serve.

beef wraps

Serves 4

Start these delicious beef wraps by cooking a sauce made of beef mince. Then simply spoon onto tortillas, and add your favourite fillings!

YOU WILL NEED

- ✓ 1 large onion
- ✓ 1 garlic clove
- ✓ 2 small red chillies
- ✓ 3–4 fresh thyme sprigs
- ✓ 1 tin (400 g) red kidney beans
- ✓ 2 tablespoons oil
- ✓ 225 g beef mince
- ✓ 1 large tin peeled and chopped tomatoes
- ✓ salt, pepper
- ✓ ½ teaspoon ground cumin
- ✓ tortilla wraps
- ✓ tortilla chips, to garnish

FOR THE FILLING
- ✓ shredded lettuce
- ✓ grated cheese
- ✓ diced tomato
- ✓ chopped onion

1 Slice the top off the onion, peel and chop it into small chunks. Wash and peel the garlic and chop.

2 Using a knife, slit the chillies open and deseed them. Rinse the thyme sprigs, and pull the leaves off the stems. Chop the leaves into fine pieces.

3 Carefully remove the lid from the tin of kidney beans. Tip the beans into a colander placed over a big bowl. Rinse the beans in plenty of fresh, cold water, then let them drain in the colander.

4 Heat the oil in a large saucepan. Add the chopped onion and garlic and fry over medium heat for about 5 minutes, until the onion is transparent (see-through). Stir from time to time with a wooden spoon.

5 Add the beef mince to the pan. Squash larger pieces with the back of your spoon. Fry, stirring, until the meat turns from pink to brown.

6 Add the chillies, kidney beans and the tinned tomatoes. Season with salt, pepper, cumin and thyme. Stir everything to mix well. Simmer the sauce for 30 minutes on a low heat, stirring from time to time. Place a dollop of meat sauce in the middle of each tortilla. Top with lettuce, cheese, diced tomato and chopped onion, and roll up the tortillas. Serve with tortilla chips.

TOP TIP

There are hundreds of different chillies. Some are very mild, others are extremely hot. Use only the amount a recipe calls for so you don't make your dish too hot to eat!

Guacamole

Serves 4

Guacamole is a delicious and creamy-smooth avocado dip. It can be eaten with tortilla chips, along with salsa and sour cream.

YOU WILL NEED

- ✓ 2 firm tomatoes
- ✓ 1 small onion
- ✓ 1 small red chilli
- ✓ 2–3 ripe avocados
- ✓ 4–5 tablespoons lime juice
- ✓ a pinch of salt
- ✓ 1 handful of fresh coriander

TOP TIP

Avocado flesh turns brown very quickly if it is not used. To prevent this, squirt some fresh lemon or lime juice all over the flesh.

1 Rinse the tomatoes under cold water. Cut them in half and remove the stems. Using a spoon, scrape out the seeds and then chop the flesh into small cubes. Peel and chop the onion and chop the chilli.

2 Cut the avocados in half lengthwise, cutting all the way around. Twist the halves in opposite directions so that they come apart. Carefully push the point of the knife into the stone, turn the knife and pull out the stone.

3 With a tablespoon, scrape the avocado flesh out of the shells. Put the flesh in a blender with the lime juice and blend. Add the tomato, onion and chilli. Season with a pinch of salt.

TOP TIP

Make your own chips by stacking a few tortillas, and cutting them into wedges. Spread out the wedges on a baking sheet, and leave for 30 minutes. Then put on a wire rack, and bake in an oven preheated to 180°C for 15 minutes.

4 Wash the coriander sprigs and pat the leaves dry with some kitchen roll. Pull the leaves off the stems, and chop the leaves with a knife. Stir most of the chopped coriander into the guacamole, and sprinkle the rest on top. Serve with tortilla chips.

National festivals

Mexico has many national festivals. Some are religious, and some celebrate events in Mexican history, such as Independence Day.

Independence Day

The most important national holiday is Independence Day. It is celebrated on 16 September, the day that Mexico remembers the fight to become an independent country. On 15–16 September 1810, a priest named Miguel Hidalgo rang church bells in the town of Dolores. He urged people to fight against the Spanish, who had ruled Mexico for 300 years. Mexico won its freedom on 28 September 1821, after the War of Independence. Today, people wave the Mexican flag and celebrate with huge parades, brilliant fireworks displays and lively dancing. There are also rodeos, bullfights and family fiestas with plenty of home-made food!

Fireworks are set off in front of the National Palace in Mexico City to celebrate Independence Day.

DID YOU KNOW?

Partygoers from all over the world come to Mexico to celebrate the carnival in Mazatlán, on the west coast. It is the third largest carnival in the world, after those in New Orleans and Rio de Janeiro.

Day of the Dead

The Day of the Dead, or *Dia de los Muertos*, is a popular holiday in Mexico. Part of a three-day festival from 31 October to 2 November, the Day of the Dead honours people who have died and mixes Aztec and Catholic beliefs. Over these three days, it is believed that the souls of dead ancestors come back to visit and guide living relatives. People visit cemeteries and tend the graves of loved ones. They light candles and bring flowers and the dead person's favourite foods. Some people stay at the graveside all night. The skeleton symbol is everywhere, even in food! Sweets shaped like skulls are popular, as is "bread of the dead", *pan de muerto*. In processions, people wear skeleton make-up and costumes.

Let's Cook!

Native Mexicans perform traditional dances at the annual Guelaguetza festival, in Oaxaca. ➡

Local fiestas

Mexicans love to celebrate! Local fiestas are held in every village, town and city across the country. Some are in honour of a local saint, but others date back to before Christianity and celebrate the harvest or the coming of the rains. There are processions around the church, lively music and fireworks. Native peoples do special dances in traditional costumes. Rodeos, bullfights and carnival rides are also common. Delicious food is sold everywhere, and home-made food is cooked to share with family, friends and neighbours.

Musicians play at the Holy Cross festival in Valle del Maiz, San Miguel de Allende, in central Mexico. It is held at the end of May each year.

Holy Week plays

In Mexico, each day of Holy Week (*Semana Santa*) leading up to Easter has a special celebration. It is popular for people to stage Passion Plays, where the last days of Jesus Christ are re-enacted. There are processions on Good Friday, but Easter Day itself is celebrated quietly.

Actors re-enact the life of Christ during a traditional Easter Passion Play procession in Tlalnepantla, in central Mexico.

DID YOU KNOW?

As part of the Holy Week celebrations, some people explode papier-mâché figures of Judas. Christians believe that Judas betrayed Jesus, which led to his death.

Three Kings' Day

Although Christmas Day is celebrated in Mexico, it is on 6 January – Three Kings' Day (*Dia de Reyes*) – that children receive gifts. The day honours the Three Wise Men who went to find Jesus after his birth. It is the wise men who hand out presents, not Santa Claus! A special cake called *rosca de reyes* is baked with a figurine of the baby Jesus inside. Whoever finds the figure must throw a party on 2 February, Candlemas (*Día de la Candelaria*), another church holiday.

Kings' cake

Makes 1 cake

This fruitcake is baked to eat on Dia de Reyes, "Kings' Day", on 6 January. It is a yeast cake that uses candied fruit in Christmas colours.

YOU WILL NEED

- 800 g plain flour
- 18 g fresh yeast
- 40 g caster sugar
- 120 ml warm milk
- 115 g softened butter
- a pinch of salt
- grated zest of 1 organic orange
- grated zest of ½ organic lemon
- 115 g mixed candied fruit, plus more for decorating
- butter for greasing the baking sheet
- 1 large egg

PLUS
- a small baby doll or other small baby figure

1 Place a flour sifter over a large bowl. Add the flour, and sift it into the bowl. This will make the flour extra-fine. Make a hollow in the middle of the flour mound with a spoon.

2 Crumble the yeast into a small bowl or cup, and add 15 g sugar and all of the milk. Stir well and pour the yeast mixture into the hollow in the flour. Sprinkle a little flour on top. Take a clean tea towel and cover the bowl. Leave it to stand in a warm place for about 20 minutes.

3 Add the rest of the sugar, the softened butter, salt and grated orange and lemon zest to the bowl. With clean hands, mix all the ingredients together. Knead the dough until it becomes smooth.

4 Using a sharp knife, chop the candied fruit. Stir it into the dough. Shape the dough into a thick ring. Put a little butter on a piece of kitchen roll and use it to grease a baking sheet. Place the dough ring on the sheet and cover it with a clean tea towel. Leave it in a warm place for 30 minutes.

5 Preheat the oven to 180°C. Crack the egg and separate the egg yolk from the white. Beat the yolk with a fork and brush it over the cake. Press pieces of candied fruit into the dough for decoration. Bake the cake for 30 minutes, then remove it from the oven. Put it on a wire rack to cool. Put the doll on top before serving.

DID YOU KNOW

The baby figurine represents baby Jesus hiding from King Herod. Around the time Jesus was born, King Herod ordered that all male babies under the age of two should be killed.

Tamales

Serves 4

This dish is made with seasoned chicken and masa harina flour. It is wrapped in a corn husk and tied with string, then steamed!

YOU WILL NEED

- ✓ 480 g masa harina flour
- ✓ 240 ml chicken stock
- ✓ salt, black pepper
- ✓ 85 g shortening or butter
- ✓ 2–3 chillies
- ✓ 450 g chicken breast, boned and skinned
- ✓ 1 onion
- ✓ 2 tablespoons oil
- ✓ 2 garlic cloves
- ✓ 1 tin tomatoes (400 g)
- ✓ 1 teaspoon ground cumin
- ✓ 1 handful fresh coriander
- ✓ softened corn husks

1 Put the masa harina flour in a bowl, add the stock and salt, and stir together until it is a thick mixture. In a small frying pan, melt the shortening or butter and stir it into the mixture. When it has cooled, knead the dough. Cover with a clean tea towel, and set it aside.

2 Rinse, trim and deseed the chillies. Using a sharp knife, cut the chicken into very small cubes. Using a clean knife, peel and chop the onion. Rinse the coriander, shake it to dry and then chop the leaves.

TOP TIP

Before you start cooking, put the corn husks into a bowl filled with warm water. Soak the husks for 1–2 hours to soften them. If you can't get any leaves, use aluminium foil instead, but don't soak it!

5 On a big plate, lay out the corn husks. Put 1½ tablespoons of corn dough on each leaf, and spread it using the back of a spoon. Place 1½ tablespoons of the chicken filling on top. Seal the dough over the chicken, then fold the husks over the dough – roll up one way, then turn up the sides and tie with a piece of string.

6 Fill a large saucepan 5–7 cm deep with water and bring to a boil. Line a steamer basket with more corn husks, and add the tamales. Put the basket in the saucepan, and cover. Simmer for 1 hour over low heat. The tamales are done when the husks come off easily.

3 Put the oil in a large saucepan, and gently heat. Add the chopped onion and fry for 5 minutes until it is golden, stirring constantly. Add the chicken and fry for 5 minutes, stirring, until the meat is brown all over.

SAFETY TIP

Always wash your hands with soap and warm water after handling raw chicken. Wash all cutting boards and utensils used to prepare raw chicken too.

4 Peel the garlic. Push it through a garlic press over the saucepan. Stir in the chillies and tomatoes. Add the salt, cumin and black pepper. Cook for a few minutes. Stir in the coriander.

Celebrating at home

Mexicans celebrate religious feast days and family events with singing, dancing – and food. Many people decorate their houses for special occasions.

Weddings

In Mexico, weddings are huge celebrations that include the couple's extended families, friends and neighbours. The couple's "sponsors" help to plan and pay for the wedding and promise to give advice on married life. Because almost 90 per cent of Mexicans are Roman Catholic, the wedding usually takes place in a church to the sounds of a lively mariachi band. During the ceremony, the groom gives the bride 13 gold coins, symbolizing that he gives her his worldly goods and trusts her. A lasso of rosary beads is put around the couple's necks in a figure of eight. This symbolizes that their lives are joined together. A big fiesta starts as soon as the church ceremony ends!

The bride and groom leave the church after their wedding ceremony in Pátzcuaro, in western Mexico.

NOS HA
NACIDO
EL

A beautiful Christmas nativity scene stands near the altar at a church in San Miguel de Allende, in central Mexico.

A traditional mariachi band performs on stage. Mariachi bands play the music at most weddings in Mexico.

The Posadas

Christmastime brings many traditions in Mexico. Every night for nine nights before 25 December, children take part in a candlelit procession called *Las Posadas*. They walk from door to door in their neighbourhood or village, carrying a nativity crèche with figures of Joseph, Mary and the baby Jesus. Knocking on each door, they sing songs until the family lets them in. This symbolizes the Holy Family being turned down at many inns until they finally reach the manger where Jesus is born. On Christmas Eve, fireworks are set off to announce Christ's birth. The *Las Posadas* tradition dates back to the 1500s and also has roots in an earlier Aztec winter solstice festival.

DID YOU KNOW?

Some brides wear a traditional Mexican wedding dress. Others wear a long white dress with a mantilla veil. Yellow, blue and red ribbons are sewn into the bride's slip for good luck, so that there will always be food, money and passion!

Birthdays

In Mexico, family and friends gather for a huge birthday fiesta. No party would be complete without hitting the piñata, a papier-mâché animal with sweets inside. People take turns hitting the brightly coloured animal until it breaks apart and all the treats pour out. The birthday meal is prepared with foods such as tortillas with salsa, taquitos (rolled tacos) and burritos. Sweets include *arroz con leche* (Mexican rice pudding), caramel flan and churros (a long doughnut). Traditionally, the birthday person's hands are tied behind his or her back as they take the first bite of the birthday cake – usually it gets squashed on their face!

A boy gets ready to hit an animal piñata at a birthday party. He is blindfolded to make it harder and more fun!

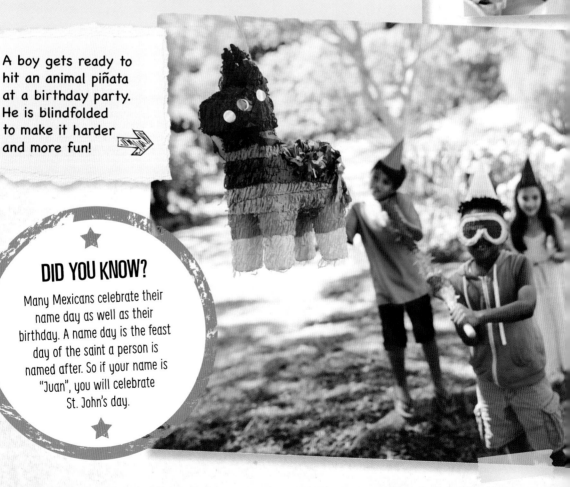

DID YOU KNOW?

Many Mexicans celebrate their name day as well as their birthday. A name day is the feast day of the saint a person is named after. So if your name is "Juan", you will celebrate St. John's day.

A Mexican girl gets ready to share her colourful Quinceañera birthday cake.

The Quinceañera

When a girl reaches the age of 15, she is considered to be a woman. The girl plans months ahead for the Fiesta Quinceañera ("party for 15 years"). She looks forward to the party with great excitement and chooses a beautiful dress and tiara. A mass is held in her honour at church, where she walks to the altar with her parents and a maid of honour. The girl offers flowers to the Virgin Mary, who represents womanhood in the church. Afterwards, there is a huge party with lots of food, special gifts and a special, lavishly decorated birthday cake!

Native ceremonies

In Mexico, some Native peoples, such as the Maya and the Aztec, combine elements of their old religions with Catholicism. They perform ceremonies that start in church, with lit candles and pine needles strewn across the floor. Then they move outdoors to perform a ritual in the caves and mountains where their ancestors worshipped. Many Maya communities still have "day-keepers", who keep track of the ancient Maya calendar, which includes a schedule for special days.

A woman performs a traditional Maya ceremony. Many of the old rituals are still performed today.

piñata

Makes 1 piñata

Birthdays in Mexico usually involve hitting a piñata until it breaks and showers everybody with sweets! This piñata takes a few days to make, so start early.

YOU WILL NEED

- 1 large, oval balloon
- two or three old newspapers
- white glue
- scissors or craft knife
- tape
- piñata patterns for the head and legs
- thin cardboard
- coloured tissue paper

FOR THE FILLING
- sweets of your choice

1 Rip the newspapers into strips about 2.5 cm x 12.5 cm. Pour the glue into an old bowl, and soak the paper strips in the glue. Blow up the balloon and tie a knot at the end.

TOP TIP
Be sure to use wrapped sweets to fill the piñata, so that they don't get stale or dusty before you play the game.

5 Fill the body of the piñata with sweets through the hole left when you cut out the lid in Step 3. Afterwards, carefully tape the lid in place.

6 To start the game, blindfold a player. Turn him or her around a few times, and give them a stick. Point them in the right direction, so they don't hit anyone! Each player may hit the piñata three times. When it breaks, share the goodies.

2 Place strips of gluey paper on the balloon until the surface is covered. Leave to dry. Repeat this three more times, leaving each layer to dry.

3 With the help of an adult assistant, cut a lid in the side of the papier mâché-covered balloon. Pop the balloon and remove it through the opening. Using the piñata pattern, draw around the outlines of the head and leg shapes onto thin cardboard, and cut out the shapes. Follow the instructions included with the piñata pattern to tape the head and legs to the body.

4 Cut the coloured tissue paper into strips about 2.5 cm x 5 cm. Glue one end of each strip to the piñata and let the other end hang loose. For the next row, overlap the strips like a row of roof tiles.

RECIPE: Let's cook!

Piña colada

Makes 4–6 cocktails

Many kinds of tropical fruit grow in Mexico, including the tangy pineapple used in this recipe. This is a non-alcoholic take on a famous cocktail.

YOU WILL NEED

- ✓ 1 small fresh pineapple
- ✓ 250 ml sweetened coconut cream
- ✓ 250 ml cold milk
- ✓ lots of crushed ice

DECORATIONS
- ✓ pineapple slices
- ✓ long straws

1 Peel the green leaves off the pineapple. Chop off the top and bottom of the pineapple so that it can stand upright by itself.

2 To cut off the thick skin, carefully slice down the sides of the pineapple. Slice the pineapple into quarters, from the top down. Carefully cut out the hard centre, and discard it. Cut the quartered pineapple into smaller pieces.

TOP TIP

Make crushed ice easily using an ice crusher. Just fill it with ice cubes, and turn the handle to crush the ice. If you don't have an ice crusher, put the ice cubes in a ziplock freezer bag, and place it on a hard surface. Bash the bag with a hammer or mallet.

5 Stir the pineapple puree into the coconut milk mix. Add crushed ice to some tall glasses, and pour the drink over the ice. Stick a pineapple chunk on each glass to decorate, and serve with a straw.

TOP TIP
You can buy presliced fresh pineapple chunks from a shop to save time preparing the pineapple.

3 Put a few pineapple chunks aside to use for the garnish. Put the other chunks into a blender, or blend with a handheld blender, to make a smooth puree.

4 Put the coconut cream and the milk into a clean measuring jug. Using the handheld blender, mix them together until they foam a little.

Daily life in Mexico

Life in Mexico's major cities revolves around industry and commerce. In the countryside, people farm the land using traditional methods. Wherever they live, 46 per cent of Mexicans live in poverty.

The countryside

People live simply in the Mexican countryside. In small villages, many families work on nearby farms, and their children join in the work. In some Native American areas, houses are made of adobe – a kind of clay material hardened in the sun – with thatched roofs. Many Native peoples make and sell crafts that their families have made for centuries, such as reed figures, handwoven fabrics and clothes and silver jewellery. Most villages have a church and a market that sells locally grown fruit and vegetables. People visit larger towns, which have more shops and national chains, if they want to buy other household goods.

A village market sells fresh produce from the surrounding farmland. People shop for fresh food in markets like this all across Mexico.

High-rise buildings spread out for miles across Mexico City. The city was built on the site of Tenochtitlán, the ancient Aztec capital that was destroyed by the Spanish in 1521.

City life

Life in Mexico's urban areas is very busy. People in cities, such as Mexico City, Guadalajara and Tijuana, work in industries including information technology, banking, textiles, shoes, medical equipment and food processing. With over 20 million people, Greater Mexico City has a subway system, buses and trolleybuses, but cars still cause massive air pollution. Wealthy areas sit next to extremely poor areas, and thousands of homeless children roam the streets.

DID YOU KNOW?

Most Mexicans have ancestors who were a mix of Spanish and Native American. This is known as being of mestizo heritage. Native peoples today include the Náhuatl, Maya, Zapotec, Mixtec and many others.

People sell goods at a busy street market on the Plaza de la Constitucion, in Mexico City.

Let's Cook!

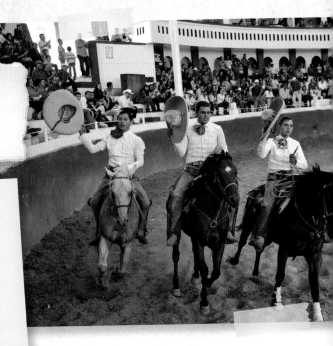

Cowboys wave to cheering crowds at a rodeo show in Mexico. Rodeos came to the country from Spain in the 1500s.

Time off

People are generally sociable in Mexico and like to spend time together. They often visit a local park, lake or beach with friends and family and take a picnic! They also visit museums and attend concerts or explore the ancient temples built by the Aztec and Maya. Football (*futbol*) is popular throughout Central and South America. People play it in parks and in the streets and cheer on the national team. Rodeos (*charradas*), where cowboys lasso and ride bulls, are another favourite pastime!

A family gathers for lunch, which is the biggest meal of the day. It is eaten mid-afternoon, followed by a siesta.

DID YOU KNOW?

Mexicans make a sauce called mole, which includes chillies, spices, tomatoes — and chocolate! It is often used in meat dishes.

38

School days

Basic education in Mexico is free for all children. Between age three and five years, children may go to nursery. But starting at six years old, they must attend six years of primary school, followed by three years of junior high school. After that, children may stop attending school, but just over half go on to study three years of high school. The school day is split into two shifts – students attend either a morning or an afternoon shift. Because it is very hot in Mexico, a two-hour siesta, or rest break, is taken at 2.00 p.m.

Children do their homework in a computer room at a village hall in Aguascalientes, a city in north central Mexico.

Mealtimes

Meals in Mexico are a chance to enjoy home-made food and share plenty of lively talk. Breakfast (*el desayuno*) is often just a sweet roll or fruit. Lunch (*la comida*) is the big meal of the day, eaten at around 2:00 p.m. It includes soup or salad, meat, seafood, or chicken and vegetables with rice or beans. A light supper (*la cena*), eaten at 8:00 p.m. or later, is usually just soup or tacos. Hot tortillas are eaten with almost every meal!

Eggs ranchero

Serves 4

This egg and tortilla dish makes a wonderful, nutritious breakfast before school. It is quick and easy to make but best of all delicious!

YOU WILL NEED

FOR THE GARNISH
- ✓ avocado and lime wedges
- ✓ crumbled feta
- ✓ fresh coriander leaves

FOR THE TORTILLA DISH
- ✓ 250 ml tomato salsa (from a jar)
- ✓ 4 wheat or corn tortillas
- ✓ 15 g butter or 1 tablespoon oil for frying
- ✓ 4 eggs
- ✓ 30 g grated cheese (for example, cheddar)
- ✓ salt and pepper

1 Prepare the garnish first. Peel the avocado, scoop out the stone and cut the flesh into wedges. Cut the lime into wedges, and squeeze one wedge over the avocado. Crumble the feta into a small bowl. Rinse the coriander leaves, and set them aside.

TOP TIP

To make your own salsa, heat 2 tablespoons oil in a frying pan. Add 1 chopped onion and 1 crushed garlic clove. Fry for 5 minutes, stirring from time to time. Stir in a 400-g tin of chopped tomatoes. Crumble 5 dried chillies, and add to mix with ½ teaspoon salt. Simmer for 10 minutes.

2 Add the salsa to a small saucepan, and simmer over low heat, stirring. Put each tortilla on an ovenproof plate, and heat in a microwave for 1 minute. Spread salsa over each hot tortilla.

4 Preheat the oven to 180°C. Sprinkle grated cheese on top of the tortillas. Season with a little salt and pepper.

5 Put the eggs ranchero plates in the oven for 5 minutes, or until the cheese melts. Garnish with the avocado and lime wedges. Sprinkle with feta and coriander.

3 Heat the butter or oil in a frying pan over medium heat. Crack one egg into the pan and fry until it is set. Using a spatula, carefully lift out the egg and place on top of the salsa.

DID YOU KNOW

Eggs are a great source of high-quality protein. They also provide 18 vitamins and minerals. Use them in baking, cooking or eat them on their own!

black bean soup

Serves 4

Forget about tinned soup – home-made bean soup is the best! This savoury dish is a meal in itself, and it is surprisingly easy to make.

YOU WILL NEED

- ✓ 1 x 400 g tin black Mexican beans (or adzuki beans)
- ✓ 950 ml vegetable or chicken stock
- ✓ 2 green chillies
- ✓ 3 onions
- ✓ 2 garlic cloves
- ✓ 450 g fresh tomatoes
- ✓ 4 tablespoons vegetable oil
- ✓ small tin sweetcorn
- ✓ a pinch of salt, black pepper
- ✓ 1 teaspoon ground cumin
- ✓ 2 tablespoons vinegar
- ✓ fresh coriander leaves

1 Put the beans and the stock in a large saucepan, and simmer for around 10 minutes over low heat. Rinse, trim and deseed the chillies. Peel and chop the onions and the garlic.

2 Put the tomatoes in a bowl. Cover with boiling water. Leave them for 1 minute. Drain and cover them with cold water. When cooled, drain and remove the skins. Cut out the stems and discard, and chop the flesh.

4 Let the beans cool a little, and ladle half the beans and their liquid into a blender, and blend them. Return the blended beans to the other beans. Stir in the onions and garlic.

5 Add a few tablespoons of cold water if the soup is too thick, and stir well. Taste to check the seasoning, then simmer the soup over low heat. Ladle into bowls, sprinkle with the coriander leaves and serve.

3 Heat the oil in a large saucepan, and add the chopped onion and garlic. Fry for 5 minutes, or until transparent (see-through). Add the chillies, the chopped tomatoes and the sweetcorn. Sprinkle in the salt, pepper, cumin and vinegar. Stir to combine all the ingredients.

TOP TIP

You can use dried beans for an even better flavour. Soak 100 g dried beans in 350 ml water for six hours. Cook the beans in a heavy metal saucepan for 1½ hours, and use in the recipe.

Mexican rice

Serves 4

This yummy rice dish makes a quick, tasty meal.
You can add pretty much any chopped vegetable,
such as peas, sweetcorn or courgette.

YOU WILL NEED

- 1.5 kg beef tomatoes
- 3 onions
- 5 garlic cloves
- 750 ml vegetable stock
- 1 tablespoon tomato puree
- 370 g long-grain rice
- 2 carrots
- 1 green pepper
- salt, pepper
- fresh coriander leaves

1 Make a slash in the top of each tomato, and plunge them into a bowl of boiling water for 1 minute. Lift them out with a slotted spoon and cool in cold water. Remove the skins, and roughly chop the flesh.

2 Peel and roughly chop the onions and garlic cloves. Put the onion, garlic and tomatoes in a blender and blend together until smooth.

3 Put the stock in a large saucepan, and stir in the tomato puree. Add the tomato, onion, and garlic mixture. Simmer until the mixture boils. Add the rice and stir well, bringing the pan to a boil again. Cover the saucepan, and simmer for 10 minutes.

4 Rinse the carrots, and scrape them clean. Rinse the pepper, cut it in half and scrape out the seeds. Slice the carrots and the pepper into long strips, then slice them into small cubes.

5 Add the carrot and pepper cubes to the rice in the saucepan. Stir everything to combine. Cover with the lid, and cook for another 10 minutes.

6 Check to see if all the ingredients are done. The vegetables should be a little crunchy. Check the seasoning. Put the rice in a bowl, sprinkle with coriander leaves and serve.

DID YOU KNOW

Rice was brought to Mexico by the Spanish in the 1500s. It has become a staple in the Mexican diet and is used in soups, main dishes and sweet desserts.

Glossary

avocado the fruit of a tree native to Mexico, with creamy, green flesh

cacao the bean-like seed from which cocoa and chocolate are made. Its origins are in Mexico. It was introduced to the rest of world by the Spanish.

carnival festivities held before Lent, usually in late February or early March

fiesta in Spanish-speaking countries, a religious festival or an event with celebrations and festivities, such as dancing and parades

guacamole a dip made with mashed avocados, chillies, lemon or lime juice, onions, tomatoes and spices

mariachi a traditional musical band that plays at weddings and festivals

masa harina a flour made from maize, or corn, used to make tortillas

piñata a large, hollow papier-mâché object containing sweets and gifts

posadas a traditional carol-singing walk made each night for nine days leading up to Christmas

quinceañera a girl's fifteenth birthday, when she is said to become a woman. She and her family attend mass, and they throw a huge party in her honour.

rosca de reyes kings' cake, made for Three Kings' Day, or the Epiphany. Traditionally, the cake has a figurine of the baby Jesus baked into it.

salsa any kind of sauce, but often a spicy dip made with tomatoes, chilli, onions and coriander

Semana Santa Holy Week, the week before Easter, celebrated in Mexico with processions and Passion Plays that re-enact Christ's last days on Earth

siesta a rest or nap taken in the afternoon during the hottest hours of the day in places with a hot climate

tamales a dish made with meat and vegetables wrapped in cornmeal, then wrapped in corn husks and steamed

tortilla a thin, round flatbread made from masa harina flour. Hot tortillas are eaten with almost every Mexican meal.

Find out more

Books

Mayas, Incas and Aztecs
(DKfindout!)
(DK, 2018)

Mexico
(Food and Cooking Around the World),
Rosemary Hankin (Wayland, 2015)

Mexico Unpacked,
Susie Brooks
(Wayland, 2016)

Websites

www.geographia.com/mexico/mexicohistory.htm
Visti this website to learn about Mexico's history and culture.

www.kidskonnect.com/Mexico/MexicoHome.html
This website has lots of interesting facts about Mexico,
including its festivals and its food.

mexicanfood.about.com
Go to this website for information about Mexican food
and cooking, as well as recipes to try.

Index